American Shorthair Cats

by Grace Hansen

Abdo
CATS
Kids

abdopublishing.com

Published by Abdo Kids, a division of ABDO, P.O. Box 398166, Minneapolis, Minnesota 55439.

Copyright © 2017 by Abdo Consulting Group, Inc. International copyrights reserved in all countries. No part of this book may be reproduced in any form without written permission from the publisher.

Printed in the United States of America, North Mankato, Minnesota.

102016

012017

THIS BOOK CONTAINS RECYCLED MATERIALS

Photo Credits: Alamy, Depositphotos Enterprise, Glow Images, iStock, Shutterstock, Thinkstock

Production Contributors: Teddy Borth, Jennie Forsberg, Grace Hansen

Design Contributors: Dorothy Toth, Laura Mitchell

Publisher's Cataloging in Publication Data

Names: Hansen, Grace, author.

Title: American shorthair cats / by Grace Hansen.

Description: Minneapolis, Minnesota : Abdo Kids, 2017 | Series: Cats. Set 2 |
     Includes bibliographical references and index.

Identifiers: LCCN 2016944064 | ISBN 9781680809183 (lib. bdg.) |
     ISBN 9781680796285 (ebook) | ISBN 9781680796957 (Read-to-me ebook)

Subjects: LCSH: American shorthair cats--Juvenile literature.

Classification: DDC 636.8/22--dc23

LC record available at http://lccn.loc.gov/2016944064

Table of Contents

American Shorthair Cats

The American Shorthair is perhaps the perfect cat. It is great at catching mice. It is also beautiful and easygoing.

4

American Shorthairs have powerful bodies. Their strong legs make them good hunters and jumpers.

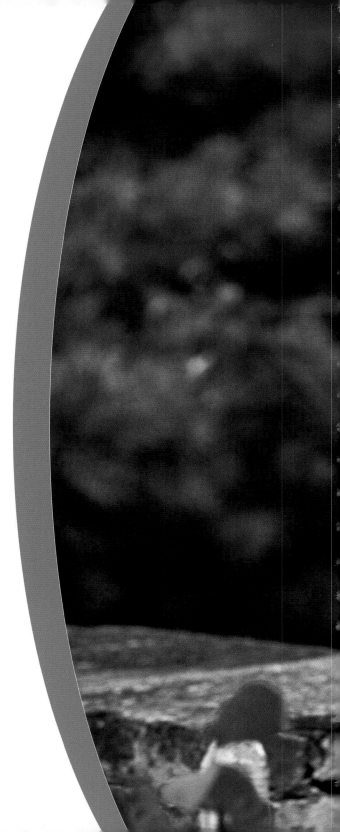

This cat's eyes and head are large and round. Its eyes can be blue, green, gold, or hazel. Its wide-set ears are rounded at the tips.

American Shorthairs have short, thick coats. Their coats come in many colors and **patterns**. The silver tabby is a common color and pattern.

American shorthairs have more hair in the winter months. This keeps them warm. They shed this extra hair in the spring.

Grooming & Food

This cat's short coat does not require lots of **grooming**. But brushing a few times a week helps with shedding. This also keeps the coat healthy.

American Shorthairs love to eat! It is important to measure their food. This will keep them at a healthy weight.

Loving, Yet Independent

This cat **adores** its family. But it is not one to cuddle a lot. It is happy just being near its loved ones.

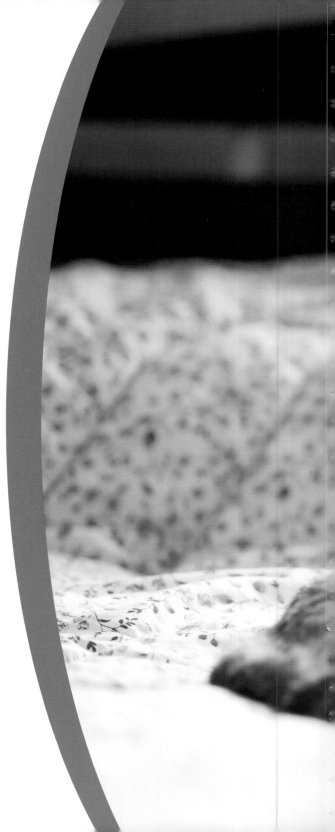

American Shorthairs are playful and smart. They enjoy playing games with their owners. But they never demand too much attention.

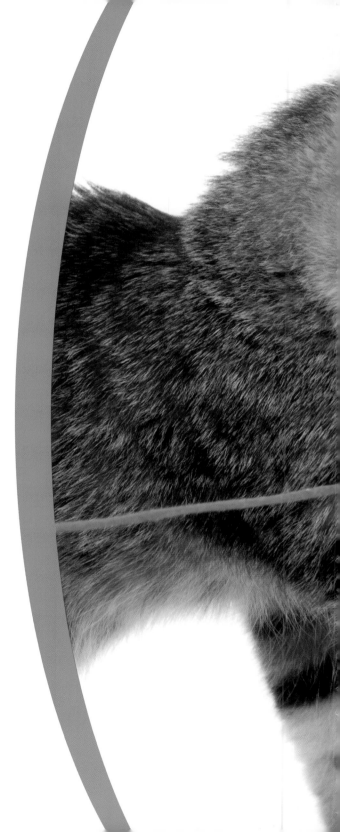

21

More Facts

- It is probably not a good idea to have an American Shorthair cat and a rodent (like a hamster or guinea pig) in the house. These cats are made for hunting!

- The **ancestors** of this cat came to the United States by ship. Their job was to clear homes and farms of pesky mice and other rodents.

- American Shorthairs come in more than 80 colors and **patterns**!

Glossary

adore – to love and respect deeply.

ancestor – someone or something that lived years ago that is related to a certain person or animal living today.

grooming – look after the coat of a cat by brushing and cleaning it.

hazel – a reddish-brown or greenish-brown color.

pattern – a repeated marking.

wide-set – positioned far apart.

Index

abdokids.com

Use this code to log on to abdokids.com and access crafts, games, videos and more!

Abdo Kids Code:
CAK9183